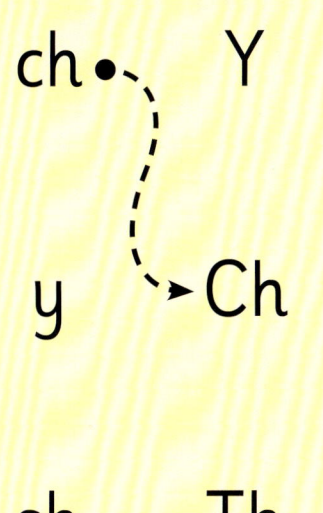

Dad and Max need three eggs and six mushrooms.

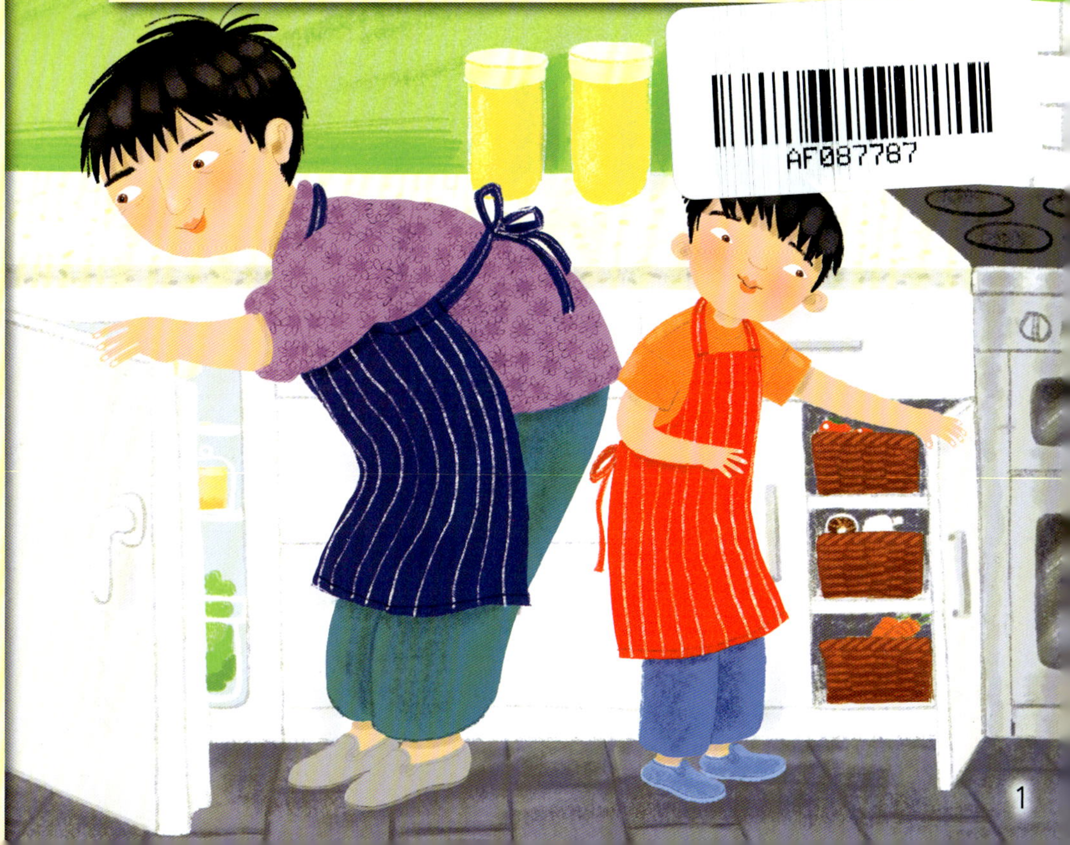

- a big pan
- a wooden spoon
- a balloon whisk
- six mushrooms
- six fresh eggs in a box

Dad chops mushrooms. Chop, chop, chop!

Max gets three eggs...

Smash! Max drops an egg!

Dad and Max mix eggs and mushrooms.

Max and Dad have omelette with sweetcorn and rocket for lunch.

Yum or yuck?

☺☹ mushrooms
☺☹ rocket
☺☹ sweetcorn
☺☹ eggs
☺☹ omelette

th X

sh Th

x Y

ch Sh

y Ch

This is Boxfish.

Boxfish is meeting Shrimp for lunch.

Boxfish fixes Crab's shell with string.

Eel is stuck in thick weeds.

Boxfish sees his chum, Shrimp.

But Haddock's Shack is shut!

Boxfish and Shrimp cannot have lunch!

'Thanks, Chicken!' Fox Cub yells.

Next morning, Fox Cub feels unwell.

Fox Cub has a rash, too.

Doctor Yak tells Fox Cub's mum that Fox Cub must rest his throat.

'Rest is boring!' thinks Fox Cub.